I0141090

POETIC LICENSE

Jack Canfora

BROADWAY PLAY PUBLISHING INC
224 E 62nd St, NY, NY 10065
www.broadwayplaypub.com
info@broadwayplaypub.com

POETIC LICENSE
© Copyright 2016 by Jack Canfora

Cover photo by Carol Rosegg

I S B N: 978-0-88145-660-8

First printing: April 2016

Book design: Marie Donovan
Page make-up: Adobe Indesign
Typeface: Palatino
Printed and bound in the U S A

POETIC LICENSE received its world premiere in September 2008 at the New Jersey Repertory Company (Artistic Director, SuzAnne Barabas; Executive Producer, Gabor Barabas), in Long Branch, NJ. The cast and creative contributors were:

KATHERINE GREER .... Anna O'Donoghue
EDMUND .... Douglas Scott Sorenson
DIANE GREER .... Nancy Ringham
JOHN GREER .... John Little

Director .... Evan Bergman
Set design & properties .... Jessica Parks
Lighting design .... Jill Nagle
Costume design .... Patricia E Doherty
Sound design .... Kevin Siwoff
Technical director .... Quinn K Stone
Assistant technical director .... Lea Anello
Stage manager .... Rose Riccardi
Assistant stage manager .... Miriam Cortez
Master electrician .... Anthony Calicchio

POETIC LICENSE received its New York premiere by The Directors Company (Michael Parva, Artistic/Producing Director; Leah Michalos, Managing Director); in association with New Jersey Repertory Company (SuzAnne Barabas, Artistic Producer; Gabor Barabas, Executive Producer) at 59E59 Theaters, running from 9 February to 4 March 2012. The cast and creative contributors were:

KATHERINE GREER ....Natalie Kuhn
EDMUND.. Ari Butler
DIANE GREER ....Liza Vann
JOHN GREER .... Geraint Wyn-Davies

Director...Evan Bergman
Scenic design...Jessica L Parks
Costume design .... Patricia E Doherty
Lighting design .... Jill Nagle
Sound design....................................John Emmett O'Brien
Casting...Judy Henderson, C S A
Production stage manager ....Rose Riccardi
General manager... Leah Michalos

CHARACTERS

KATHERINE GREER
EDMUND
DIANE GREER
JOHN GREER

"Children begin by loving their parents; after a time they judge them; rarely, if ever, do they forgive them."
Oscar Wilde

"The blood jet is poetry—there is no stopping it."
Sylvia Plath

"When I was a child, I spake as a child, I understood as a child, I thought as a child: but when I became a man, I put away childish things."
Corinthians 13:11

Scene I

*(Lights up to reveal a well-appointed living room. It is
clear from the decor of this room that its owners have the
wherewithal to make it opulent but have the sophistication
not to. Impressively stocked bookshelves flank the room. U S
C is a window large enough for an adult to squeeze through
if he or she so chose. After a moment, a woman so chooses.*
KATHERINE *pushes open the window and starts her struggle
into the room. She is about twenty and an attractive,
aggressively bright young woman. This method of entry into
the room is not foreign to her, yet is still achieved with a
large degree of inelegance. She flops down into the room and
then gathers herself.)*

KATHERINE: There. Well, that brings back a few
memories. *(She goes to the window.)* Now you try.

EDMUND: *(Offstage)* I can't climb this.

KATHERINE: Sure you can. A teenage girl could climb
this. A teenage girl has climbed this, in fact. Many
times. Drunk. In heels.

(After a moderate offstage struggle, we see EDMUND *flop
his way into the room. Twenty-six and not uncoordinated
by nature, he is not quite used to flailing about as helplessly
as the window's entry demands. He has a knapsack on his
back.)*

KATHERINE: I like the way you almost did that with
dignity.

EDMUND: *(Playful)* And I like the way you almost went thirty seconds without being a pain in my ass.

KATHERINE: *(Smiling, playful too)* I know, that would've been a new record. I was cheering you on. In my own way.

EDMUND: By mocking me.

KATHERINE: Well, one should stick to one's strengths, I feel. Besides, I was actually very supportive—I didn't point out once when you were climbing just now—though climbing is a strong word for what was going on—how you were clearly pretending to be like, James Bond the whole time.

EDMUND: *(Finding a spot for knapsack—still playful with her)* No I wasn't.

KATHERINE: It's not your fault; it's innate. Anytime a man does something clandestine and physical like that he pretends he's James Bond. It's a biological fact. Saw it on Nova.

EDMUND: Most families find the front door more efficient.

KATHERINE: That's my bad. I didn't bring my key—my parents are never out, usually.

EDMUND: Have you tried their cells?

KATHERINE: *(Laughs)* My parents relationship with technology is frankly Amish. Can't have gone far—they'll be back soon. Climb would've been easier, by the way, if you'd left the knapsack outside with our other stuff. No one's going to steal it.

EDMUND: You're right.

KATHERINE: It's a pretty upscale neighborhood; I think your toothbrush and underwear would be safe. Unless you're fostering some creepy new Linus/blanket dialectic we should discuss.

EDMUND: Well, you know, I've got some other stuff in there, too; you know, books.

KATHERINE: Ah, yes, "your poetry".

EDMUND: It's amazing how good you are at putting quotation marks around words with just your tone of voice. Like every time you say "your poetry".

KATHERINE: It's a useful post-modern skill. Make you a deal: let me read it, show me it exists, and then I won't have to put it in quotes any more. Hell, if you're lucky I may even start saying it in italics, like: *your poetry.*

EDMUND: Problem is, my stuff's hardly italics-worthy.

KATHERINE: Well, how would I know?

EDMUND: Whereas yours is.

KATHERINE: You're sweet and, it should be noted, very perceptive.

EDMUND: So some of that's in here, too; and some other stuff.

KATHERINE: Well if it's got my poetry, by all means never let it leave your sight. *(She kisses him, deeply and sincerely. Beat. Smiles)* It's weird that you're here.

EDMUND: Is it?

KATHERINE: Well, subjectively weird, anyway. I get it makes all the sense in the world empirically. And it's not that I'm not excited about it; I am. I just mean in the, um, taxonomy of my life, you know—"you" and "here" are totally distinct ecosystems.

EDMUND: Distinct but compatible, no? Ecosystems adapt, right?

KATHERINE: *(Smiles)* Yes.

EDMUND: Didn't you tell your parents you were coming back tonight?

KATHERINE: Sort of.

EDMUND: Sort of.

KATHERINE: I told them we were coming. But early tomorrow, not tonight.

EDMUND: Why?

KATHERINE: One day you'll laugh that you could ask such a question.

EDMUND: Seriously, Kath—

KATHERINE: It's never a good idea to let her know exactly when you're coming. When they get here, we'll make up something about not being able to catch a bus tomorrow or something. She'll be a little pissed but it's better than the alternative.

EDMUND: The alternative being not lying to your mother?

KATHERINE: The alternative being she would have prepared this unspeakable charm offensive. It's like Amanda Wingfield on a coke binge. She'll still be embarrassing, but the element of surprise will dilute it a bit. I hope.

EDMUND: You know everyone's always a little embarrassed by their folks and there's almost never a need.

KATHERINE: But there are embarrassing people in the world, Edmund. Many of whom have children. So, statistically speaking, some of us are right. It's a little white lie; it's not like I'm Dick Cheney. Are you nervous or something?

EDMUND: Well, you know, breaking and entering has that effect on me. And I've always found—you know— meeting the parents a little nerve wracking but, you know, I've been on their property for three minutes and I've already committed a major felony.

KATHERINE: Don't be nervous.

EDMUND: You're nervous. *(Playful)* Hypocrite.

KATHERINE: I'm not a hypocrite, I'm *layered.* You should totally relax.

EDMUND: Really? You orchestrated our arrival like a ransom drop and you live here.

KATHERINE: Well, of course I'm nervous; I thought it was understood you were going to be the calm, nurturing one in our relationship so I could have the latitude to be as fucked up as I deemed necessary at any given time. And, for the record, I'm nervous about you meeting them, not them meeting you. There's a big difference. Besides, I don't live here. I live with you now.

EDMUND: Yes and I can't wait until that comes up at the dinner table.

KATHERINE: It won't, it won't. And that'll be fine, by the way, for the ten thousandth time. They are educated, open-minded people who treat me, by and large, more or less like an adult. This is my fault totally. I'm sorry I've got you all worked up about my mother. I'm sure to the untrained eye she appears quite harmless.

EDMUND: I'm actually—to be honest, I'm actually more tense about meeting your father.

KATHERINE: God, —you wouldn't say that if you knew him. He's so unintimidating it's astounding. I mean, he's a genius, but you know, totally chill about it.

EDMUND: Well, that sets my mind completely at ease.

KATHERINE: He's really just— *(She searches for a word to capture his essence, falls short, abandons the effort.)* —he's great—you'll see. Why are you suddenly so nervous about meeting Dad?

EDMUND: Oh, you know, you're his little girl, blah blah blah, the usual Freudian smorgasbord. Plus, none of my other girlfriend's father's had a Pulitzer on his mantle.

KATHERINE: He doesn't keep it on the mantle. He's pretty self-conscious about it, in fact. Of course, that doesn't stop my mother mentioning it twelve times whenever she calls for dinner reservations. She can't ride his coattails very far if he's sitting in his study. She's relentless. Booking lectures or, or getting him to write essays and lend his name to—and I worry about him. Not, you know, tragically—it's not like he's a Bronte sister or anything, but it, it takes its toll, her um, managing of things. You'll see. Not this weekend, hopefully, but you'll—I mean it takes its toll on me and I'm—believe me—very much on the periphery.

EDMUND: I'm sure that's not true.

KATHERINE: *(She smiles at* EDMUND.*)* By the way, don't bring up the whole Laureate thing yet. My father would be embarrassed and my mother, well, it's not official yet, so until we get word, she's very tight lipped about it—it's the only thing on earth, Christ knows, that she is tight lipped about. Although, I have to say, I find the fact that you're nervous about telling them we live together very sweet. In an anachronistic, woman—as—chattel, petty bourgeois sort of way.

EDMUND: Which is very sweet of you. In a smug, condescending—to—my—values, over-privileged sort of way.

KATHERINE: Which is why we work so well together.

EDMUND: *(Looking around the room: the bookcases)* Hey, how tough was it for you growing up with him as your father? Like with your friends at school and stuff?

KATHERINE: Not very, Edmund, he's a poet—it's not like he's Bono. Are you nervous about meeting him because he's a great writer, or because you're passionately smitten with his daughter and you're desperate to meet a man who gave the world such a ravishing creature?

EDMUND: The second thing.

KATHERINE: You are a smart one. (Half playful, half in earnest) You should at least let him look at your poetry.

EDMUND: Yeah, that's exactly what I'm going to do.

KATHERINE: It's important for him to help young writers. He's very helpful with my stuff.

EDMUND: 'Cos you're his baby.

KATHERINE: No, no. He's my father and he's very supportive. But. He has high standards. Higher for me than others sometimes, it feels like. Which I—I appreciate that. It's a sign of respect.

EDMUND: Yeah.

KATHERINE: We know each other too well to bullshit anyway, especially about writing. He's always respected me enough to be totally honest. And the truth, you know, as they say, is sometimes… but it's helped me, my writing, he's helped me enormously; he really has. Last year or so especially. I've improved—and a lot of it is him. He's been great about it. Supportive and…and so, when he really likes something, I'll know it's good. I mean truly. I'll know. Beyond any shadow of a—and that's a pretty great thing to have.

EDMUND: Yeah.

KATHERINE: And these new ones, about the farmhouse? I'm kind of—well, not proud but, I feel sort of relatively OK about them. Ought to. Made like three thousand revisions.

EDMUND: Listen to me: they're very good. I've read a lot of, I keep telling you, a lot of poets—young poets—

KATHERINE: The tragic curse of the English graduate teaching assistant.

EDMUND: Not just that, no. And yours are...very good.

KATHERINE: I don't know about the "very." But I'll take it.

(We hear a parents coming home sort of noise.)

KATHERINE: Here they come. *(She takes his head in her hands. Gives him a quick kiss. Smiling but earnest)* I'm sorry I'm so disproportionally freaked about this. And I'm sorry that I'm gonna freak out once or twice again this weekend. But that's, you know, just my shit. Not ours, right?

EDMUND: Right.

KATHERINE: Right. *(She kisses him.)* Good. Glad that's cleared up.

(The first parent to enter is KATHERINE's mother, DIANE. She invariably sweeps into a room rather than enters it. She has been drinking a bit but her behavior often suggests this, so KATHERINE does not immediately notice it.)

DIANE: Hello sweetheart, you're here early, what a wonderful surprise! *(She embraces and kisses KATHERINE.)* You look beautiful. Thin but beautiful. Of course, girls today have been brainwashed into thinking the two words are synonymous—models today all look like Dachau inmates with makeovers. I wish you wouldn't allow yourself to be conned in to that.

KATHERINE: I haven't been conned. This is my natural weight.

DIANE: When you were seven it was your natural weight.

KATHERINE: No, that's not—

DIANE: Well, it's your natural weight if you live on a diet of caffeine and water, I'll give you that. Doesn't she look too thin, Edmund? This is Edmund, isn't it? Quite an awkward moment if it isn't.

EDMUND: Yes, I'm Edmund.

DIANE: Well, one catastrophe averted. It's a pleasure to meet you. We've heard so many wonderful things about you—not literally, of course, because Katherine never tells us anything about her life that actually matters to her—we were lucky to get your name out of her—so her total silence on the subject of you bodes something quite serious, I would think. I suppose what I should've said is that we've inferred great things about you.

EDMUND: Well, um…thank you. It's very nice to meet you. Katherine talks about you often.

DIANE: (Impressed and amused) "Talks about you often." How deftly phrased. He's a clever one, sweetheart. Hang on to him. Very clever. He's even managed to avoid answering my question so far. Wouldn't she be prettier with an extra ten pounds?

KATHERINE: Is there a way he could answer that without alienating at least one of us?

DIANE: Not if I've phrased it right. I'm joking of course, Edmund; don't pay any attention to me—you'll get the hang of that after a while—I'm sure Katherine's briefed you fully on me on the way down but—in my defense—I mean well. Of course, the road to therapy is paved with good intentions, right sweetheart?

KATHERINE: How are you, Mom?

DIANE: Put out, to tell you the truth. Your Aunt Sarah and Uncle Don canceled at the last minute.

KATHERINE: Really? Why?

DIANE: God knows. Who can listen to a woman who uses the phrase "up the wazzoo" on a regular basis? Some song and dance about her sciatic nerve. Her nerve, my ass. So naturally your cousins won't be coming down either.

KATHERINE: No?

DIANE: Naturally. And your Aunt Debbie cancelled yesterday.

KATHERINE: Oh.

DIANE: Which really is just as well as I couldn't get my hands on the amount of Prozac needed to slip into everyone's water supply to make 48 hours of her bearable. So, everyone's out, basically—the whole family's disappearing—we're dropping like Kennedys around here.

KATHERINE: Is Dad upset?

DIANE: Who can tell? I doubt it. He wanted a very small celebration for his birthday. Well, small he wanted, small he got.

KATHERINE: Oh.

DIANE: I'm sorry?

KATHERINE: I said "oh".

DIANE: Ah. Anyway—Edmund—you must be parched after the long climb up the window—what can I get you to drink?

EDMUND: I'm fine, thanks.

DIANE: Well don't hesitate—make yourself at home—although you strike me as too polite to feel comfortable doing that so I'll just check in with you periodically—how's that?

EDMUND: It's fine, sure.

KATHERINE: *("Let's back off a little, now, please")* Mom.

DIANE: I'm simply being a polite hostess. Whatever you'd like Edmund, is fine by me. But you have to promise not to be shy and let me know, O K?

EDMUND: Promise.

DIANE: You're a sweet boy. I can tell already. I hope you and Katherine work out. That's exactly the sort of thing that Katherine lives in mortal terror of me saying—but it's what I feel, so why not, right? Why shouldn't I?

KATHERINE: And another chapter in my memoir's just written itself.

(JOHN GREER *enters.* EDMUND, *standing near his knapsack, subtly touches it.*)

DIANE: You're here just in time to save your daughter from further embarrassment at her mother's hands.

JOHN: I'm sure that's not true.

KATHERINE: Hi Dad. How are you?

(KATHERINE *hugs* JOHN *warmly.*)

JOHN: Fine, sweetheart, fine. Your mother said you'd be here tonight.

KATHERINE: Did she?

JOHN: Yes; sorry we weren't here to greet you. *(To* EDMUND*)* Hello.

EDMUND: Hello, nice to—

KATHERINE: We weren't supposed get—where were you two anyway? You're never out.

JOHN: Oh…some function of the Dean's. We felt we should put in an appearance. *(Trying to acknowledge* EDMUND*)* How do you—

DIANE: Because—he typically fails to mention—because this little function of the Dean's was in your father's honor.

JOHN: No, no, not just me, no. There were other writers there, too. From our department. One's quite good actually. I'd hoped it would help get his work some attention.

DIANE: Whatever, John, it was in your honor. You think over two hundred people would've shown up to hear about what's his name's book?

JOHN: Kevin Dineen.

DIANE: Well, whatever. They weren't there for him, my dear. It's not his birthday they're celebrating. There were over two hundred people there, not including media.

KATHERINE: Media?

DIANE: Yes, darling. Plural of medium.

JOHN: My dear, it's a college campus. If there's was free food and alcohol you can get two hundred people to show up at a party celebrating the birthday of Josef Stalin.

DIANE: Well, belittle it all you want, P B S was thrilled with it. They're going to use it in their piece.

KATHERINE: P B S's doing a piece on you?

JOHN: Yes, well, your mother seemed to feel it would—

KATHERINE: Mom, why would you—

DIANE: Wait a minute—you cannot lay this on me—this is so typical of you—she's been home two minutes and already I'm the bad guy.

KATHERINE: Was this your idea?

DIANE: That's not the point.

KATHERINE: That's not the point? I thought we'd discussed this weekend as just a family thing—*family*—no events, or—just once, I wish you'd suppress the urge to make our lives a, a *reality* show for English majors.

DIANE: That's not what this—John?

JOHN: What exactly is a "reality show"? Is the oxymoron intentional?

KATHERINE: He's pushed enough as it is, don't you think?

JOHN: Sweetheart—

DIANE: Oh for the love of—he's not exactly on his feet for fifteen hour shifts assembling iPhones for you and your friends, since you're such a champion of the oppressed—

KATHERINE: I'm talking about Dad right now.

DIANE: This will re*duce* his workload, actually.

KATHERINE: Somehow I'm skeptical about that.

DIANE: They wanted him to go on a—tell her, John—

JOHN: I was supposed to go on a month long book tour, sweetheart, for this anthology I've edited, and I was dreading it, just dreading it. I couldn't—they replied I had to, and so on and so forth until it started to become quite acrimonious when your mother suggested this piece as a compromise. F B S, in an apparent attempt to make their other programming look commercial in comparison, has been trying to get me to do this thing with them for awhile.

DIANE: Yes. (DIANE *mimics an imagined commercial for the documentary)* "You thought his poems were boring—wait until you meet the man!"

JOHN: Something like that, I'd imagine. The point is, this way, P B S gets their show, the publishers get their requisite publicity, and I get to stay home.

(JOHN *motions towards* EDMUND *and is about to introduce himself when* KATHERINE *speaks.)*

KATHERINE: They're not coming here, are they?

JOHN: Who, sweetheart?

KATHERINE: The T V crew or whoever. Because when we spoke about this weekend we'd agreed—

JOHN: No. Not tonight. Not this weekend. We were— your mother was firm about that.

KATHERINE: Good.

(Pause. Off of DIANE'*s stare:)*

KATHERINE: What?

DIANE: Looking back on this, if you're ever wondering, the words you should have been searching for were: "Thanks, Mom. Well done."

(DIANE *storms out. Pause)*

JOHN: Katherine…

KATHERINE: What did I—I didn't do anything.

JOHN: I'm not saying you did, but from your mother's perspective, she worked quite hard to get us this weekend free from them—not because she cared, but because she knew you would. A subtle expression of gratitude would go a long way, I think.

KATHERINE: It's not exactly that easy.

JOHN: Which is why it would go a long way.

KATHERINE: I'll…try. I will.

JOHN: Thank you. There seems to be a young man standing in my living room. To whom does he belong?

KATHERINE: Oh God, I'm sorry. I'm just…anyway, Dad, this is Edmund.

JOHN: It's a pleasure to meet you, Edmund.

EDMUND: How do you do, sir.

JOHN: Please don't be so formal. My daughter's said so little about you that I'm sure we'll be seeing a lot of each other. Call me John.

EDMUND: All right.

JOHN: Good. Katherine, the longer you wait to try and make amends with your mother, the steeper the climb it becomes. Perhaps you could go into the kitchen and calm her down.

KATHERINE: I can't think of a person less qualified for the job.

JOHN: That's where you're wrong, sweetheart; it's simply never been a field that's interested you much. You know how…excitable your mother can become after these social functions—I think it would mean a lot to her if you made the gesture. It would certainly mean a lot to me. I'm sure I can talk with Edmund here for a moment or two without embarrassing either of us too egregiously.

KATHERINE: All right—you're—I'll go. *(She exits.)*

JOHN: Can I offer you something to drink?

EDMUND: I'm fine, thanks.

JOHN: Katherine and her mother are similar in many ways, so naturally they find each other irritating from time to time. I suspect most families share the dynamic, don't you?

EDMUND: I'm sure you're right.

(Pause)

JOHN: Certain reactions become so ingrained for them I doubt they're even aware of it half the time. But Katherine, I think I can say objectively, is a remarkable young woman and so, I'm sure you're a remarkable young man.

EDMUND: Yes, well—I think she's remarkable, too.

JOHN: Glad to hear it. Please, please, have a seat. How rude of me.

EDMUND: Not at all.

(Pause)

JOHN: I'm doing a very poor job, aren't I?

EDMUND: Of what?

JOHN: Of putting you at ease.

EDMUND: I look uncomfortable to you?

JOHN: No, no, it's—I remember meeting Katherine's mother's parents, remember it like it was a half an hour ago. Very nerve wracking.

EDMUND: Was it?

JOHN: Oh God yes, of course. Desperate to make a good impression. Katherine's grandfather was a fairly well known publisher, and I was—well it's a nightmare scenario for a parent—I was a poet. Never much took to me, despite my best efforts, I'm afraid.

EDMUND: Why is that, do you think?

JOHN: I'm not sure. But you know, every family's a foreign country. Impossible to understand all the nuances of the native culture. Anyway, I'd like you to know if Katherine likes you, and she obviously does, then I think I'm bound to, too.

EDMUND: That's nice of you to say.

(Pause)

JOHN: Events like tonight aren't my favorite way to spend an evening. My hope is I can at least help a few other writers out at these things. I mean…the fact is, you reach a certain age when you realize that you've been very lucky. There are a lot of writers out there who are probably just as good as me, probably better in fact, but…like anything else, you need a little luck in life. Regardless of talent, regardless of…you need a little luck. And I've had a lot of it. To reach the level of recognition I've been able to reach. So, anything I can do to help…God I couldn't be more pompous and boring right now, could I?

EDMUND: Not at all.

JOHN: You're kind, but I was. Forgive me. Even I stopped listening to me half way through.

(DIANE and KATHERINE enter.)

KATHERINE: Mother, you're being—

DIANE: Shh! Edmund, your girlfriend is spreading nasty rumors about you in the kitchen claiming you're a vegetarian.

EDMUND: I'm afraid that's true.

KATHERINE: I'm a vegetarian, too.

DIANE: Oh, Katherine, don't be ridiculous.

KATHERINE: What's ridiculous about being a vegetarian?

DIANE: Nothing—fine, fine, be a vegetarian if you think it will—

JOHN: I'm sure it's not an inconvenience at all, Edmund.

DIANE: Yes, I was just getting to that. It's not an inconvenience. I can whip up some extra vegetables—

EDMUND: Oh, I'm sure there's no need to—

DIANE: Absolutely. You don't think we weren't going to feed you, did you?

KATHERINE: It's a little late for a meal, Mom.

DIANE: Of course it isn't.

JOHN: Actually, Katherine—I think it might be nice to unwind over a light supper. Of course, if you and Edmund are too tired after your trip…

EDMUND: No, no that's very—I'd be delighted. It'll be nice, right, Kath? Family dinner.

DIANE: Absolutely; and of course it'll give us the chance to subtly interrogate you—John, where did we put the index cards?

KATHERINE: Mother—

JOHN: Sweetheart, Edmund may not yet be accustomed to your lambent wit. I promise no motives other than hunger.

KATHERINE: Sure. Let's get our stuff, Edmund.

EDMUND: Our stuff?

KATHERINE: *(Irritated that he hasn't picked up on her subtext of "I want to talk to you alone")* Yes. Outside. By the window. Let's get our stuff. Together.

EDMUND: *(He gets it now)* Oh. Sure. O K.

KATHERINE: We'll be right back.

DIANE: We'll be right here.

KATHERINE: I know.

(EDMUND *and* KATHERINE *exit. Pause)*

JOHN: She's tense.

DIANE: Oh, I hadn't picked up on that.

JOHN: I know you know.

DIANE: Well, as long as I know you know I know. *(Beat. She smiles.)* You were good tonight. At the reception.

JOHN: You think so?

DIANE: Very good. I know you hate those things, but they're important. I hate them, too.

JOHN: *(Laughs)* You *thrive* in them.

DIANE: Doesn't mean I don't hate them. *(Sighs)* I'm tense, too, for the record.

JOHN: I know. Me too. But we're not tense about *this.* Or very tense, anyway.

DIANE: You're right. *(She goes to the bar, fixes them both a drink.)* The waiting is getting to me.

JOHN: Me too. Did Jeff tell you—did they give any indication of when we can expect they'll—

DIANE: They told me that we could expect a call—

JOHN: On second thought, don't tell me. I want to be on a need to know basis about all this political nonsense, and I don't need to know.

DIANE: *(Smiling)* No, you don't. *(Hands him the drink)* I've been trying to think the past couple of days—I've been trying to picture what Dad would have said.

JOHN: About?

DIANE: *About?* About—

JOHN: Being named Poet—

DIANE: Ah ah—no jinxes Yes.

JOHN: *(Smiles)* If I recall, he managed to take the news of my Pulitzer without bursting any buttons on his vest.

DIANE: He *was* proud. That's not fair.

JOHN: O K.

DIANE: And this is different.

JOHN: It is?

DIANE: I don't know. I think it is, a little.

JOHN: O K. I think he'd probably say something about standards having become lax.

DIANE: *(She smiles at this. Crosses to him. A quick kiss. She rubs his shoulder)* Maybe. But we'd know better.

(JOHN smiles. Takes DIANE's hand)

DIANE: We'll—

(But KATHERINE and EDMUND have entered, and immediately JOHN crosses to KATHERINE.)

JOHN: Where are your bags?

KATHERINE: We left them in the foyer. I figured we could move them after dinner—

DIANE: Yes, yes, fine; we need to get back in the kitchen, Katherine. It'll be a nice dinner, Katherine, I promise. Besides, Edmund, you'll find us interesting, too—we can trade notes on what it's like to live with Katherine.

KATHERINE: Excuse me?

DIANE: You aren't living together, Edmund?

EDMUND: Yes…yes we are, actually.

KATHERINE: What are you, spying on me?

DIANE: Oh for God's sake, Katherine, a mother simply knows these things. Right John? I think it's very smart by the way. Can't tell a thing about a person unless you live with them. Not even then, sometimes. Sweetheart, help me with the dinner—I don't want to get a letter from PETA next week saying I used excessive force chopping the carrots. Come on, Katherine, I need your help, I'd like to eat soon, I'm starved.

(KATHERINE rather reluctantly exits.)

JOHN: I'm sorry if my wife…if she made it awkward for you just then.

EDMUND: No, not at…well, a little, yes. It's fine, though.

JOHN: But like I said before, if Katherine's happy with you…that is…well, she's young, but on the other hand she's always been older than her years. In some ways.

EDMUND: In some ways, yes.

JOHN: And Diane, well, not to belabor it at all, but Diane can…overwhelm people sometimes a little at first, but she has a lot of wonderful qualities, too.

EDMUND: Yes, I'm sure.

JOHN: She's not nearly as…well, indiscreet as she can seem.

EDMUND: Oh yes, I know.

JOHN: You know?

EDMUND: Oh yes.

JOHN: How do you mean?

EDMUND: Well, I mean, she's obviously kept quiet to Katherine about a few things concerning you.

JOHN: I'm sorry?

EDMUND: My guess is she has a ton of discretion. I mean, I've only been fucking your daughter for a couple of months, and I've had to bite my tongue a bunch of times not to let the cat out of the bag about you.

(KATHERINE *enters.*)

KATHERINE: All right boys, let's go, dinner's almost served. Come on, come on, I exhausted all semblance of small talk before the napkins were folded. I need you two, let's go.

(KATHERINE *comes between* EDMUND *and* JOHN *and, linking her arms with one of each of theirs, leads them off to the dining room.*)

(*Blackout*)

Scene II

(*The same living room about an hour later. Two pairings—* DIANE *and* EDMUND, *and* JOHN *and* KATHERINE *enter the room.* DIANE *is laughing and enjoying the conversation as well as the bottle of wine coursing through her blood.* KATHERINE *seems more tense than ever.*)

DIANE: Passable, I would think, yes?

JOHN: More than that, my dear. More than that.

KATHERINE: Very good, Mom. It was very good.

DIANE: It's the sauce; it's all in the sauce. Anything is palatable if you've got it in the right sauce, I always say.

EDMUND: It was very good. Delicious, it was very kind of you to—

DIANE: Well you're kind; you're under a certain obligation to say nice things about it, obviously, so we have to take it with a certain grain of—but I really think—it's funny, too, sometimes I can spend hours—I have, haven't I, John? Spend forever in the kitchen trying to get the proportions just right and sometimes I do but as often as not something's a little off—too much salt, and like tonight, where I'm not even thinking about it, don't bother to measure or—and it's perfect! Well, not perfect, —but it was, you know, sort of just throw it together, hodge podge and it comes out fine anyway. They say though, you know, that the best chefs never bother with measuring; they just sort of, I don't know, feel their way through the meal. God

I wish it were that easy for me, you know? But, you know, the sauce, how bad can—you can't go wrong with a good sauce.

KATHERINE: Yes, I think you've made it clear how much you enjoy the sauce.

DIANE: Have I? I have I suppose; I'm sorry. I feel rather silly now.

JOHN: No, not at all, you shouldn't feel—

DIANE: Although I suppose that was the point. I'm sorry…I must have—

EDMUND: No, no, not at—I cook a little, too. I've heard that, too, about the chefs. The top ones not measuring things out in cups or anything.

DIANE: Are you more a measurer or a feeler, would you say?

JOHN: I'm guessing you tend to measure, Edmund.

DIANE: Really?

EDMUND: Yes, that's true, I measure every time.

DIANE: Really? Why?

EDMUND: Oh, gosh, my stuff's barely edible when I stick to the recipe, right Katherine?

KATHERINE: You have other qualities working for you.

JOHN: I'm sure.

DIANE: Katherine, get me another glass of wine please.

KATHERINE: You want another glass of wine?

DIANE: How quickly you pick up on things. I told you all the money we spent for the private schools would pay off one day, John. I'm not driving anywhere tonight darling, for Christ's sake.

KATHERINE: Yes but you are planning on walking later tonight I'd assumed.

JOHN: Katherine...

DIANE: Katherine, don't be such a Puritan; it doesn't suit you. "Dost thou think, because thou art virtuous, there shall be no more..." um, shit. I'd be able to get the line sober ironically.

JOHN: "Cakes and ale..." my dear.

DIANE: Thank you. "...do you think there shall be no more cakes and ale?" That's the line, right? I'm sorry, dear, if I've been such a—I suppose I'm a little...giddy, tonight. I'm just very happy to have you back. I know it's inconceivable to you, but I miss you tremendously while you're gone.

JOHN: That's very true.

DIANE: I'm just happy to have you home is all. And to meet Edmund. It's such a relief, frankly. Isn't it, John?

EDMUND: *(Quickly, smoothly)* Well, that's nice of you to say. How so?

DIANE: You should see the parade of troglodytes Katherine's trooped through these doors. Her last boyfriend had so many piercings his body made a whistling sound if he moved quickly.

KATHERINE: All right, fine.

DIANE: More shrapnel than personality, that one. Still, what's the point in being seventeen if you can't shock the parents by dating a project from shop class? I'm embarrassing you again, aren't I?

KATHERINE: *(All of this is clearly not fine.)* No, it's fine.

DIANE: I don't mean to embarrass you.

KATHERINE: You're not.

DIANE: Yes I am; I can tell. Edmund, I'm sorry if I've made you uncomfortable.

EDMUND: No, not at—

JOHN: Edmund isn't uncomfortable.

DIANE: I mean, I hope I didn't embarrass you by drinking wine at dinner, God forbid. I know how decadent that is.

EDMUND: Not at all. "Good wine is a good familiar creature."

DIANE: Thank you. How's that for quoting Shakespeare, sweetheart? It is Shakespeare, right?

JOHN: Yes. Iago, I believe.

EDMUND: That's right, yes.

KATHERINE: The line is actually— "Good wine is a good familiar creature if it be well used." It's not the concept of wine at dinner I'm objecting to here, obviously…

DIANE: Oh it's my drinking wine at dinner.

KATHERINE: No, it's—

DIANE: For Christ's sake, darling, why can't we have a nice, relaxing evening? You've been coiled like a spring all night.

KATHERINE: I'm not—

JOHN: Well, it's been a long day for her, darling; traveling always makes me anxious, too.

(By now DIANE has gone over to KATHERINE and attempts to massage her shoulders as if to say "Relax" —KATHERINE is not interested.)

KATHERINE: I'm fine.

DIANE: I'm just trying to get you to relax and enjoy yourself is all. Everyone's having a nice time.

KATHERINE: Yes, fine.

DIANE: Keep quoting Shakespeare, Edmund, you'll be sure to get in good with the old man, right John?

JOHN: Yes, well, admiring Shakespeare hardly puts me at the cutting edge of literary criticism, I'm afraid.

DIANE: I didn't say it did, did I? I only said you liked him.

JOHN: Of course.

KATHERINE: Edmund's an expert on his work.

JOHN: Oh yes?

EDMUND: No, no.

KATHERINE: Your senior thesis was on his problem plays, wasn't it?

EDMUND: Well, yes, but undergrad.

DIANE: Very nice. What was your major?

EDMUND: Theater.

DIANE: No, really, what was it?

KATHERINE: Mother.

DIANE: Oh, just a good natured joke, Edmund. Theater. I mean, why not get a degree in Phrenology while you're at it?

KATHERINE: She's only joking, Edmund; she happens to have a lifelong love of the theater. She's often urged Dad to try his hand at playwriting.

DIANE: Because I'd hoped the rehearsals would get him out of the house.

EDMUND: Yes, thanks again for dinner tonight. Very hospitable of you. Everything was great.

DIANE: Well, in any event, I had a lovely time. I did. A cozy, intimate evening. Dinner with my husband, my daughter and her live in lover.

KATHERINE: Jesus.

JOHN: Diane…

DIANE: Am I wrong?

EDMUND: I, I wouldn't call it that.

DIANE: Why not?

KATHERINE: Can we not be this dramatic about it? You're going to make like it's a big deal?

DIANE: It is a big deal. But it wasn't a reproach. I didn't mean it disapprovingly, Edmund, I'm sorry if it seemed that way.

KATHERINE: How else could it seem? Jesus.

JOHN: Perhaps a less…aggressively descriptive term would be preferable.

DIANE: All I was…whatever. You—you're the poet; you're the one who's paid to be vague—

KATHERINE: Mother—

DIANE: So let me know whatever euphemism you coin and I'll commit it to memory. I meant no offense.

EDMUND: None taken.

DIANE: I will not repeat the phrase again, now that I've been corrected. By everyone. How nice. It's simply the term we used back in the Dark Ages. One reason I never gave in to plastic surgery; I knew my slang would always give my age away.

EDMUND: It's fine, honestly, it's O K.

KATHERINE: Speaking of poetry, Dad, did you take a look at…I mean, you've probably been too busy to—

JOHN: No, not at…

KATHERINE: I feel bad even—

JOHN: No, no, sweetheart, I'm sorry…I did look at the ones you sent me. The three poems, yes? The ones about…about the barn or…

KATHERINE: *(Simultaneous with "barn")* Farmhouse—
yes.

JOHN: Farmhouse, yes. Yes. Like I said, I haven't
been—I've been a little swamped with this anthology,
but yes, I was able to—they're, parts of them I think are
quite solid, I think. You know? Tough to tell from first
drafts sometimes, naturally. But good. Some of it. Yes.
Quite.

DIANE: Well, that's the sort of rave book jackets are
made of.

KATHERINE: I'm not looking for a compliment, Mom. I
don't…that won't help me. What didn't you like?

JOHN: No, no, I didn't say it wasn't…it's not as if I
didn't like it, you see. I did.

KATHERINE: *(Simultaneous with "like it, you see")* No,
you're right, …they're kind of…generic, I know…kind
of…they're competent, you know…

JOHN: Yes. Very, abso—

KATHERINE: And that advice you gave last time—about
condensing—I tried that—

JOHN: Helpful?

KATHERINE: Oh yes—*totally*—and I think it worked.
You know… *(Pointing to a specific part of the page)* …the
economy of it here.

JOHN: *(Looking at that part)* Oh yes. Yes, very. That's
very nice, that part.

KATHERINE: So I'm, um, I'm working at it, you know?
Trying to—

JOHN: Oh yes, sweetheart, absolutely. That's clear.

KATHERINE: But that next…level or whatever…how do
I find that?

JOHN: Yes…well, yes. (*Small laugh*) To teach that. It would be nice if—if that could be taught.

KATHERINE: Of course.

JOHN: Sweetheart.

KATHERINE: It's O K.

JOHN: I think there's reason to feel positive about this.

KATHERINE: Yes

JOHN: This is a step. A normal step in the process.

KATHERINE: (*Over "in the process"*) I know.

JOHN: Nothing to be down about. (*A warm smile*) You should've seen some of my first drafts.

KATHERINE: Yeah.

JOHN: But that's what first drafts are for, sweetheart.

DIANE: I know I don't count in this because—well, because I don't, but I thought those poems were wonderful, sweetheart. (*Sincere*) I was very proud.

KATHERINE: (*Embarrassed but sincere*) Thanks, Mom.

DIANE: And your father was, too, right John?

KATHERINE: But I think these have—all the things we talked about last month, what you said about having the courage to—

JOHN:	DIANE:
Sweetheart, it's not that—	John, perhaps you can—

KATHERINE: Put in the things you're most embarrassed by—I think—

JOHN: Sweetheart—

KATHERINE: I feel that these address—I mean, don't you think they address that?

JOHN: Part of being a poet—sometimes the toughest part—is being able to look at your poetry honestly, right?

KATHERINE: No, I understand, it's not that I'm not willing to—

JOHN: *(A slight rise in tempertaure at having to continue this)* You can be defensive about this or learn from this. I'm showing you the respect of being honest. One poet to another. Which is what you want, right?

KATHERINE: True. Yes.

JOHN: *(His authority no longer in dispute)* Good. That's my girl. It's a good first draft. Keep at it.

KATHERINE: *(The smile willed back)* Yes.

(Pause)

DIANE: So you graduate in May, Edmund.

EDMUND: Yes.

KATHERINE: With his Masters.

DIANE: Very nice. What in?

EDMUND: Literature. American literature. Twentieth century.

DIANE: Mmmm…hear that, John? You owe the poor boy an apology. He's probably had to write papers on you.

JOHN: I'm sure I was barely mentioned at all.

EDMUND: Well, I wrote one, actually. A comparative paper between you and e.e. cummings.

JOHN: So, you've done some research on me.

EDMUND: Oh yes.

JOHN: Well, now that upsets me.

KATHERINE: Dad?

JOHN: Several hours of your life you'll never get back I'm afraid. At least you got to read some Cummings.

DIANE: Ah, the trademark modesty.

KATHERINE: You never mentioned that to me.

EDMUND: Well, that paper was back as an undergrad, actually. Seven years ago.

JOHN: Seven?

EDMUND: Yes. I'm twenty-six, actually. I—I took some time off before going for my Masters degree.

DIANE: Oh.

KATHERINE: He had to get a job to pay for it all. His mother raised him and she died when he was fourteen.

DIANE: Jesus, John, our daughter's sleeping with a Dickens character.

KATHERINE: I can't believe you said that.

JOHN: Katherine…

DIANE: Sweetheart, a joke, a joke for chrissake…

EDMUND: It's really not as dramatic as all that. I had an aunt and uncle who helped take care of me. It wasn't too bad, really.

DIANE: Well, I'm glad for that. Your aunt and uncle are still with us?

EDMUND: Yes, they are.

DIANE: Not mangled to death in Victorian era machinery or anything?

KATHERINE: Mother, stop it.

DIANE: It was a joke; I'm sorry Edmund; I was joking, I'm sorry.

KATHERINE: Stop it.

JOHN: That's enough, Katherine.

(Pause. An offstage phone rings.)

DIANE: I'll get it. Feel free to hop on the extension Katherine and make snide comments under your breath. *(She exits.)*

JOHN: You owe your mother an apology.

KATHERINE: You've got to be—

JOHN: Katherine, you can't speak to your mother like that.

KATHERINE: Don't...don't make me out to be some fourteen year old rolling her eyes in front her friends because her mother's asking if she's got a warm enough jacket on. She's drunk.

JOHN: You're exaggerating.

KATHERINE: Are you kidding me? I'm getting you a breathalizer for Christmas.

JOHN: Please honey, I...why don't you get some coffee for us. Your mother was about to and it might be a nice sort of peace offering if you helped her.

KATHERINE: Fine. I'm hopeless at it but—Edmund, help me out in the kitchen, make sure I'm not poisoning us.

JOHN: No, I want to pick Edmund's brain.

EDMUND: About what?

JOHN: Shakespeare.

KATHERINE: All right then. You boys chat away—I'll start the coffee. I've seen it done once before in a movie. *(She exits.)*

EDMUND: Lear's my favorite—how about you?

JOHN: I think you owe me an explanation.

EDMUND: Yes?

JOHN: And an apology. All through dinner I've been turning over in my head why you would try to provoke me like that.

EDMUND: Come up with anything?

JOHN: Outside of the obvious, that you're a disturbed and vulgar individual, no. I'd hoped you'd take this opportunity to explain yourself and apologize, but since it's clear there's no apology forthcoming, I've little choice but to insist you leave my house immediately.

EDMUND: Of course.

JOHN: I intend to let Katherine know exactly what you've said to me.

EDMUND: I see.

JOHN: Did you really think I would let something like that pass? It's a…it's an unfortunate side effect of today's world that when someone achieves a certain recognition, that it attracts sad, delusional elements such as yourself. That's why, what little limelight I've been afforded, I have diligently shunned.

EDMUND: The P B S documentary notwithstanding.

JOHN: I've no intention of explaining a single second of my life to you, nor of wasting a single second more of my life in conversation with you. I'll give you two minutes to collect your things and leave.

EDMUND: Here's what surprises me. You're so good with words. Economy and precision, every critic says so. And then you use a completely inappropriate word.

JOHN: I'm getting Katherine.

EDMUND: Like delusional.

JOHN: I've utterly no interest in your—

EDMUND: I will leave here and never darken your door again if you can point out to me a single thing I've said tonight that is the least bit delusional.

JOHN: Being delusional, by definition, you will be unable to recognize any instances of delusion.

EDMUND: Touché. But humor me. I mean, where's the delusion?

JOHN: You seem to think you've got something on me, or you wouldn't have implied you...I believe the cliché you used was "let the cat out of the bag".

EDMUND: That's true.

JOHN: And there's your delusion.

EDMUND: But it's true.

JOHN: And what dreadful secret of mine do you feel you have access to?

EDMUND: Do you really think I've endured three hours of your wife's semi-coherent drivel and three months of your daughter's semi-competent fellatio to make it that easy for you?

JOHN: Apparently you've endured it all simply to sling some juvenile vulgarities at me in the hopes of—I don't know exactly what you're hoping to accomplish, to be honest. I have nothing to hide from anyone.

EDMUND: Even your daughter?

JOHN: Especially my daughter.

EDMUND: I wouldn't...I wouldn't call my bluff if I were you, John.

JOHN: There are many things in my life I am not proud of, but there are none of which I am ashamed. Katherine! Come here please, right now.

EDMUND: Zora Gibson.

JOHN: What?

(KATHERINE *enters.*)

KATHERINE: What's up?

EDMUND: Settle a bet for us, Kath.

KATHERINE: You're betting on Shakespeare?

EDMUND: Sort of. "What's in a name?" Right, John?

KATHERINE: What's the bet?

JOHN: What?

KATHERINE: What's the bet?

JOHN: Nothing. Is your mother off the phone?

KATHERINE: I don't think so. What's...what's the matter, Dad?

JOHN: Nothing, hon. Tired.

EDMUND: We're keeping you up, aren't we?

JOHN: No, no, it's...fine. It's only nine-thirty, after all.

EDMUND: That's true. The night is young.

KATHERINE: Not if I don't get some caffeine into our systems it isn't. I'll be in with the coffee in a minute. How many slices do you want?

JOHN: I'm sure it's not as bad as that.

KATHERINE: I'm going to remind you that you said that. If Mom comes through here, send her in to see if she can salvage it. *(She exits)*

EDMUND: Didn't I warn you about calling my bluff?

JOHN: What do you think...what is that name supposed to mean to me, as you see it?

EDMUND: As I see it?

JOHN: Yes.

EDMUND: Well I gotta say, John, I don't see how that matters.

JOHN: No?

EDMUND: No, John. If what I thought mattered, you wouldn't be living this carefree life you've carved out for yourself.

JOHN: It isn't carefree.

EDMUND: I think you're being unduly modest. The articles, interviews, book jackets, they pretty much tell the same story: soft -spoken, humble young man publishes, in two years, three volumes of breathtaking poetry, becomes a literary icon by the time he's forty; chairs humanitarian conferences, publishes a fourth book of poetry—this time a Pulitzer winner—to cement his status in the annals of American writers, composes Op-Ed pieces for *The New York Times*, becomes a leading voice of morality and conscience for…well, for pretty much everyone.

JOHN: You're exaggerating.

EDMUND: I prefer hyperbole, John. More literary. Still, everyone sort of, you know, looks up to you.

JOHN: Is that what this is about — have you taken offense to something I've said, some position I've taken? Is this some sort of misguided political act?

EDMUND: Take offense? John, how could I take offense to your political actions? Speaking out against children getting blown up by land mines? Wanting to shelter the homeless? Not exactly much to argue with, from my perspective. No, I like your politics, John.

JOHN: Then what is…what is all of this about?

EDMUND: I told you. Zora Gibson.

JOHN: What…what about her? You've dug up a name you feel should mean something to me and try to swing it around over my head like a—

EDMUND: Tell me something—how is it with all the shit they've written about you, you've been able to keep her hidden away?

JOHN: I haven't hidden anything.

EDMUND: Well, now you're lying, and that pisses me off. I haven't lied to you have I? Honest to a fault, I'm sure you'd agree.

JOHN: You've lied to my daughter.

EDMUND: So have you.

JOHN: What do you want?

EDMUND: What do I want?

JOHN: Yes.

EDMUND: What do I want?

JOHN: I don't think I can be any plainer.

EDMUND: No, probably not.

JOHN: So?

EDMUND: Do you…I'm sorry, do you think I'm blackmailing you?

JOHN: I think you're…I think you're trying to, yes.

EDMUND: And you'd be…willing…to be blackmailed?

JOHN: There's nothing I've done that I feel merits blackmail, but…

EDMUND: But?

JOHN: What has become very clear, is that you can't—I can't allow you to stay with my daughter—that's obvious. So think of what you need to—you can blame it on me, if you wish, whatever will cause the least pain for her and the most distance from you.

EDMUND: Well good for you, John.

JOHN: So we have an agreement?

EDMUND: Oh, good fuck, no. I just think it's great how you've managed to turn this into a way of making yourself feel like a good father. I don't want your money, John. I'm not here to blackmail you.

(Pause. JOHN smiles.)

EDMUND: Something funny, John?

JOHN: Of course not. But I wonder. You've taken a certain measure of me, or you think you have, anyway. I don't know what methods you've used, of course. *(Slight smile)* Google perhaps. My daughter. No doubt even my behavior when we met. And so. That's what you know of me. You've an undeniable—if crass—sort of cunning, so I'll appeal to that part. I'm betting you're smart enough to understand that you can't possibly be smart enough to really know me. Not through those… surface things, anyway.

(DIANE enters. She is excited.)

DIANE: Well, your daughter is not going to be happy with the timing of this—no one will be, really, but you can't nitpick about a thing like this.

EDMUND: Timing of what?

DIANE: We got the call. It looks like it's going to happen.

JOHN: That was—

DIANE: Yep.

JOHN: Just now?

DIANE: Just now.

JOHN: He said—it's all been—

DIANE: Yep. It's official. Or will be Monday. Poet Laureate.

EDMUND: Well, congratulations, John.

(KATHERINE *enters with a tray with a coffee pot and sundry coffee items*)

KATHERINE: Congratulations?

DIANE: Your father's going to be named Poet Laureate on Monday.

KATHERINE: Really? Oh my God. That's so great, Dad.

JOHN: Well, thanks, sweetie, but—it's not official—anything could happen.

DIANE: What could happen, John, you're being ridiculous. It's not something they sweat too much about, sweetheart, it's not like the Joint Chiefs are playing out war game scenarios with you versus Maya Angelou. So yes, it happens on Monday.

KATHERINE: Wow.

EDMUND: That'll be pretty big news, I'd imagine. I mean, like press and stuff.

JOHN: No, no, poetry doesn't make the papers.

EDMUND: Sometimes poets do.

DIANE: It will be big news. Big news for us, anyway. P B S's very excited.

KATHERINE: Yes, I would imagine they would be. Wait—you spoke to P B S about this already?

DIANE: Well, of course—you think we should try and cover this up? Your father didn't knock off a liquor store, for God's sake, Katherine, he's being given a prestigious honor.

KATHERINE: You still told them nothing this weekend, right?

DIANE: I think things have changed a little bit—I think our plans this weekend are going to have to be flexible with this.

EDMUND: Absolutely.

DIANE: I'm so excited.

KATHERINE: Is it a lot of money?

DIANE: Not a lot. A nice bonus is all. I meant the honor of it. But the money doesn't hurt, now you mention it.

KATHERINE: Jesus.

DIANE: Yes, we know you and your father's disdain for all that smacks of commerce. Which is a luxury you both can afford because I make sure all the bills are paid. Let's just enjoy the moment—even if it is tainted with the awful prospect of having a little more money. Besides, you know I've offered many times to cut off all financial support if you feel it'll help your writing.

KATHERINE: Thanks.

DIANE: *(This is an old refrain of hers.)* Why are there so many starving poets, Katherine?

KATHERINE: *(Finishing the distasteful catechism)* Because they're not married to you.

DIANE: That's right.

KATHERINE: *(Somewhat resigned)* So what does this— what happens now?

DIANE: First of all we'll have to fly to Washington tomorrow. You should come, too, Edmund. It'll be fun, we'll get to meet the president maybe. They're going to send a car to take us to the University and meet up with everyone in a few minutes to get your father's reaction, and ours.

KATHERINE: Who is?

DIANE: What?

KATHERINE: *(Does not like the sound of this)* Who are we meeting up with?

DIANE: P B S. And the university contacted the local news stations.

KATHERINE: Why did you feel compelled to let everyone know right away? Tonight? I thought this weekend was supposed to be about Dad's birthday and meeting Edmund.

DIANE: They don't have birthday cakes in Washington? We can't talk to Edmund on a plane?

KATHERINE: Wait a minute—did you just call them?

DIANE: Yes.

KATHERINE: And they'll all be at the school waiting?

DIANE: Yes. In a little while, anyway, yes.

KATHERINE: The whole crew and everything, all the camera people and—

DIANE: I suppose so, Katherine, I don't know—should I have them e-mail a roster to you?

KATHERINE: On Friday night—this late?

DIANE: I guess so Katherine. What's your point?

KATHERINE: And the university contacted the news and everyone right away—wow—that is efficient.

DIANE: Katherine—

KATHERINE: They were told to be ready for this. Because you told them to be ready.

JOHN: Katherine.

KATHERINE: What, Dad? Like it's not true? You wanted me here because it'll look better for the fucking documentary.

DIANE: Yes, sweetheart.

KATHERINE: Jesus. And your bulllshit about—

DIANE: It is nice to live in a house full of poets—

KATHERINE: (Louder and more emphatic as a response to this) —your fucking bullshit about telling them nothing this weekend was just a lie.

DIANE: I told them nothing this weekend if it didn't happen.

KATHERINE: Which you didn't show the courtesy of telling me about by the way—

DIANE: You wouldn't have come if I'd told you that.

KATHERINE: But you knew it probably would happen this weekend.

(DIANE *doesn't answer.*)

KATHERINE: Jesus.

DIANE: Look, to be perfectly honest, we don't need you here if you're dead set against it—it would just be a nicer picture—more complete.

KATHERINE: You don't need me and yet it was still worth lying to me about.

DIANE: Oh could you please stop with the wounded child bit, it's not a big—

KATHERINE: It is to me.

DIANE: Which is precisely why you need to be handled. If you think all it takes to be a great artist is being great, then you're more naïve than I'd thought—I am doing what I need to do for the good of our family. And this is what is done. Or at least this is what is done if you want to actually get anywhere, which is something I do know about. I mean by all means find a garret somewhere in Paris if you feel I'm sullying your father and our name and your art—but just remember all those nice first editions you pulled from our oak bookcases all these years so you could feed your mind and want to be a poet and admire him and sneer at me —they were all made possible by the very things you sneer at me for in the first place. Things like this. I'm sorry you don't like it, but it's what is done. Christ, this is a strain for everyone, not just you.

KATHERINE: Oh please—what you've left out of your speech just now is that —that the least little chance to soak up some exposure and you're...you make Lady Gaga look like J D Salinger.

JOHN: Katherine...

KATHERINE: You're going to have him touring malls...

DIANE: The melodrama, my God, Edmund, I don't know how you—

KATHERINE: She's going to make me out now to be— that I just don't understand that these things come up and I have to roll with the punches; what's left out of this narrative—what's always omitted, always—is for just exactly whom all of this headlong pursuit of, of just whatever it is you're so hellbent on him pursuing in the first place is for.

JOHN: Perhaps...

DIANE: What?

JOHN: Perhaps we could point out to them that it's a bit of an imposition this weekend. Tell them —I don't know—I'm not feeling up to it.

DIANE: You're not feeling up to it? They haven't asked you bowling, John. It's an honor.

KATHERINE: It's an honor for him, not us, not me and, not to put too fine a point on it, not you.

JOHN: Katherine. I think it's for everyone in these circumstances.

DIANE: Jesus...well I—listen, we'll have to make the best of it, sorry. "There is nothing good or bad but thinking makes it so." Got that one right, didn't I, Edmund?

EDMUND: Yes.

DIANE: It is an honor for all of us. We're all a part of this—of his work.

JOHN: That's true.

KATHERINE: He wrote most of it before I was born.

DIANE: Fine then, maybe it isn't an honor for you then, if you insist on seeing it that narrow mindedly. But I have put as much—no, not as much, obviously. But I have sacrificed—

JOHN: Yes, that's true, sweetheart.

KATHERINE: How? How have you sacrificed? Dad struggles and suffers to churn out articles and essays and, and poems, has to sweat through the interviews and book tours and public scrutiny so you can keep living your life like you're on the cover of *The New Yorker*. How have you sacrificed? Enlighten us. Catalogue the indignities you've had to bear that make it standard operating procedure to lie to me so casually. Let's *hear* it.

JOHN: Katherine, let's—

DIANE: Oh my God, do you ever listen—do you need me to—believe me, sweetheart, you don't want to know.

KATHERINE: You know, I pathologize it with therapists and rationalize it with friends, you know, like any self-respecting, self-loathing woman of the 21st century; I, I try to give my, my issues with you, um, context and perspective, but that lasts about three minutes when I come here and those well meaning adult defenses have to square off in the ring with the ten foot tall fact that you are full of shit.

JOHN: Katherine, please.

DIANE: Darling—I am not, as you so eloquently put it, full of shit. But what I am full of, as you have pointed out throughout the evening with all of the subtlety of a gang rape, is wine, which is going to be real bad news for everyone in this room in about two seconds if you don't shut your—

KATHERINE: Oh, now we've reached the stage where we make vague, ridiculous threats. That's my favorite part of these evenings. Because that means the next stage is usually passing out on the couch.

JOHN: STOP IT! JUST STOP IT GODAMMIT, KATHERINE, STOP IT!

(KATHERINE, *and indeed the others, are stunned into silence*)

JOHN: Now stop it, I am asking you to…please, just…I need a minute for things…to settle.

KATHERINE: Fine. Yes, I'm sorry…I'm… *(She exits.)*

JOHN: I'm sorry…I—are you O K?

DIANE: Yes, yes, I'm fine.

JOHN: You're—

DIANE: I'm in control of myself, yes, is what you're really asking. Yes. Are you?

JOHN: What? Yes, of course. I'm sorry for…just a moment ago.

DIANE: Yes. Well, go talk to her.

JOHN: She's all right.

DIANE: She's not all right, John. You want her like that when they get here?

EDMUND: When are…

JOHN: What?

EDMUND: When are they coming?

DIANE: They said about a half hour.

JOHN: A half hour.

DIANE: Yes, so, you'd better calm her down.

JOHN: I don't want them here in half an hour.

DIANE: Well, then you call them. If you really don't want them here, you go and call them for Christ's sake. Get off your ass, get down in the trenches for once and call them, goddammit!

JOHN: That isn't fair.

DIANE: Oh fair ? Twenty five years into the marriage we're introducing fair? Going to be hard for you to keep that halo we've fitted you for balanced if you're actually going to start bending down to help, but I'm game.

JOHN: Fine, fine.

DIANE: Oh please. Fine. Don't.

(*Pause.* JOHN *imperceptibly retreats. Some delicate ground is being trod on—but* EDMUND *can't quite crack the code of* JOHN *and* DIANE*'s silence*)

DIANE: Maybe Edmund should speak to Katherine.

JOHN: No. I—I'd…I'd better go and speak to her. I'll be back in a moment.

(JOHN *exits. Awkward pause*)

DIANE: Well, you'll have to give us this—you certainly got your money's worth out of that bus ticket. Sorry about this. Not every occasion is like this, I promise. Sorry.

EDMUND: No need to be sorry. If it's any consolation, you're nothing like I pictured you.

DIANE: Should that be a consolation?

EDMUND: Not sure. But…you do know, don't you?

DIANE: Know what?

EDMUND: I wasn't sure you did, but you do, don't you?

DIANE: I know quite a few things, Edmund, I went to graduate school, I listen to a lot of N P R; you'll have to narrow the field a bit.

EDMUND: Your husband's poems. You know that he didn't write them.

DIANE: How would I…how would I know something like that?

EDMUND: I don't know. But you do. We both do.

DIANE: *(Trying to get a handle on this—is this simply his bad attempt at easing tension?)* I'm sorry?

(EDMUND *yields no reaction. Trying a new tact:)*

DIANE: Well, you're a wily one, Edmund, you've caught us. They were actually written by Sir Francis Bacon…no, wait—Kevin Bacon…no, not Kevin Bacon, but someone who knows him.

(EDMUND's *expression has not changed. A terrible realization—he's being serious)*

DIANE: You're not joking. You're really…oh, Edmund…please…don't.

EDMUND: Don't?

DIANE: Don't turn out to be crazy. If you think somehow that… *(A realization)* …are you one of those people? Oh God, you're one of those people, aren't you?

EDMUND: What people?

DIANE: You're one of those people who think it's not enough to read the novels or poems or whatever…like the one who waited outside Bob Dylan's house every night to comb through his garbage cans—

EDMUND: Really? Someone did that? That's pretty funny.

DIANE: No, Edmund, it's sick. And people like that focus so much on the minutiae they can't possibly see the overall picture clearly. Which means that inevitably they get even the basic things terribly wrong. Which is O K within limits; I mean that's why God invented graduate schools, based on what you've just said to me, I think maybe you're a garbage picker.

EDMUND: No I'm not, honestly.

DIANE: Then it's worse than that—you're an academic. Not that I should bite the hand that gags me, but… you're one of those sad people who goes around… dusting the language for fingerprints. My God, living with my daughter— Poor Katherine's going to have to take an ambulance to therapy. O K, O K, let's take this a step at a…why would you say something like that?

EDMUND: Because it's true. And I—well, you actually feel things. The only one in this house, frankly, who does. I love Katherine but she's so soaked in irony she can't get her head above the water, and John—John sniffs around every emotion like a cat pondering a fresh killed mouse.

DIANE: Jesus, is it—is that why? Because John is different from his poems? Of course he's different from his poems. That's why he wrote them down. That's why it's a talent—a skill, to make poetry of things. To concentrate feeling like that. That's why the poets always disappoint. At least the ones who don't kill themselves.

EDMUND: How much do you know about Zora Gibson?

DIANE: Zora Gibson? Wow, how did you…are you writing a book?

EDMUND: Who the hell writes a book about a poet? I can't believe there's a T V crew coming here to do something on him.

DIANE: He's about to be made Poet Laureate.

EDMUND: So I heard. Who gives a fuck? A hundred people, a hundred people with English degrees, for God's sake, you pull them in off the streets, and with a gun to their heads they couldn't tell you who the Poet Laureate is. You'd be lucky if five of them could even tell you what the Poet Laureate is.

DIANE: Maybe. But a few of them could probably tell you who John Greer is.

EDMUND: Possibly. Thanks in no small part to you. What are the odds of your husband being a writer and your father being one of those rare people who can almost single-handedly get an unknown writer published. Must have been fate. "Why are there so many starving poets? 'Cos they're not married to you." But no. I'm not writing a book.

DIANE: Then how did you dig up an obscure name that?

EDMUND: Like what?

DIANE: Zora Gibson.

EDMUND: Well, she's not obscure to me; she was my mother.

(This stops DIANE cold. Pause)

EDMUND: Well, hell, if I'd have known that's all it took to shut you up, I'd have told you at dinner.

DIANE: I don't know what to say. Have you...Christ... does John know?

EDMUND: Not that particular tidbit, no. He sure knows something's up; he knows I know her, or know her name anyway, but not that. I thought maybe you'd like to tell him.

DIANE: And what does Katherine know?

EDMUND: Katherine doesn't know anything. I'd be happy to keep it that way, too.

DIANE: Really? One is almost giddy with anticipation to see how you plan on pulling that off. Until one remembers you've most likely been full of shit all along.

EDMUND: How much she's hurt in the end has as much to do with you and John as me.

DIANE: And just how do you—

EDMUND: You're a pragmatist, Diane, right now you need to focus on John's problem.

DIANE: Why have you come here?

EDMUND: Why have I come here? Your husband steals my mother's poetry—makes a career out of her suffering—builds an ivory tower for himself and his family carved from her bones—the question you should be asking is what's taken me so long.

DIANE: Your mother's poetry?

EDMUND: I'm usually pretty good at reading people, Diane, but I haven't quite pinned you down yet. I can't tell how much you know. I mean, I've got that you're the Colonel Tom to his Elvis, but I mean how did you know about...I mean, did you ever see him write them?

DIANE: Did she tell you this? Because I knew your— well, knew of her, vaguely, anyway, and I was led to believe that she was...that she suffered from mental illness.

EDMUND: Wow, Diane, that's the first time tonight that you've tried to search for the politically correct term.

DIANE: I didn't want to—

EDMUND: No, I understand your position. "Suffering from mental illness" is preferable to "being mentally ill." Because that way the person is not consumed by their condition. They are not defined by it. You were making fun of academics just now, but that is the Mount Everest of academic bullshit. And it was what defined her. And it did consume her. Her and any person who cared about her. So when you're ten and you have to pull your mother out of restaurants and department stores every week because she's half naked and screaming at strangers, when you're twelve and you have to clean up her bed nights after she's pissed in it, when you're thirteen years old and she confuses you in mid conversation with her father, or with men she's fucked, it's a little hard not to—it just feels funny when someone says that she "suffered from mental illness". Just doesn't have the requisite stench of shit and blood and humiliation to it. So let's establish that my mother didn't suffer from mental illness. She lost her fucking mind.

DIANE: I'm sorry.

EDMUND: It's fine.

DIANE: But as she had…lost her mind, you can see why I might greet her claim about John's poetry with a bit of skepticism.

EDMUND: Absolutely, yes. But she never said anything about it.

(JOHN enters.)

JOHN: She'll be down in a minute. She's just a little overwrought. She's worried about me. Diane, I'd like to talk with Edmund alone for a—

EDMUND: She knows, John. In fact she knows more than you do.

DIANE: You'll never guess who his mother was.

JOHN: *(Realizing himself)* Jesus. And what you said about your mother passing when you were fourteen, that's true?

EDMUND: Haven't lied yet, have I? Cancer.

JOHN: Oh Christ. You're aware, obviously, that your mother and I...knew each other.

EDMUND: In the biblical sense.

JOHN: It wasn't like that...we were actually very close. For a brief time.

EDMUND: Oh my God.

DIANE: You lived with her, John. He knows. Stop dancing around everything. He knows you lived with her. He knows you left her for me.

EDMUND: Yes.

DIANE: You see, all out in the open. Better to get it over with I say, like a band-aid.

EDMUND: Let me ask you something, you left her a little while before I came on the scene...had she started to lose her mind when she was with you?

JOHN: Do you blame me—

EDMUND: Not entirely, John. Your mere absence, no matter how callous its execution, couldn't cause a meltdown of my mother's proportions. My guess is she was in a slow decay from the start.

JOHN: Yes. Well, I am sorry for everything you had to go through.

EDMUND: Don't try to spoil it with your phony compassion, please.

JOHN: Even you can't believe you're any kind of authority on the subject of compassion.

EDMUND: And why's that, you think?

JOHN: The way you've used my daughter.

EDMUND: The way I've—you know what? Your indignation would carry a little more weight if you hadn't let her shiver in your shadow all these years.

DIANE: He's done nothing of the sort.

EDMUND: You've lied.

JOHN: I've lied? Excuse me?

DIANE: Edmund thinks you stole your poems from his mother.

(Off of JOHN's *disbelieving look:)*

DIANE: He's very serious about this, John.

JOHN: And what is this based on?

EDMUND: I have proof.

JOHN: Proof? Oh my God, this is really beyond… Edmund, I…I'm sorry, I almost wish it were true, in a weird sort of way, I do. Life has been desperately unfair to you. At least I hope it has, because otherwise there'd be no excuse for you, would there?

EDMUND: I suppose not.

JOHN: But there's nothing else to say really. She didn't write them.

EDMUND: You're going to stick to that?

JOHN: Oh for—Edmund, you do make it difficult to do the right thing.

EDMUND: And what's that?

JOHN: I'm not saying I'm not still upset or…ill at ease with you. But perhaps, given what you've been thinking all these years, your behavior is perhaps slightly more understandable.

EDMUND: Well, that's awfully magnanimous of you. So brass tacks. You were talking a second ago about

the right thing to do. Here's your chance: credit my
mother.

JOHN: What?

EDMUND: For the poems she wrote. Co-writing
credit. And the "co" part of that is, for my money,
exceptionally magnanimous of me. You sit in
your chair and you smile and you talk about how
everyone "needs a little luck". Always helping other
writers. John Greer: always quick to thank so many
goddamned people. And where's my mother? Where
is she?

JOHN: Diane.

DIANE: Edmund, this is—

EDMUND: Credit her. That way Katherine will know at
least that much truth. And I promise you she'll never
hear about the rest—how you used my mother, for her
poems, abandoned her to her illness, none of it...credit
her. And then I'll disappear from all of your lives.

From hers. She'll be rid of me with nothing more than
garden variety heartbreak. Credit her.

DIANE: My God, this is your plan?

EDMUND: My mother, after all you did to her, after all
she did for you, deserves at least that much.. Tick tock.
They'll be here any minute. Agree?

(KATHERINE *enters, unseen by the others.*)

JOHN: Edmund, listen to me. No matter how much you
want this to be true, it isn't. And I know your mother
wouln't try deliberately to mislead or—I knew your
mother—

EDMUND: Yes.

KATHERINE: How do you know Edmund's mother?

JOHN: It's a, quite a, yes, it turns out I knew Edmund's mother.

KATHERINE: Oh my God, really Edmund?

EDMUND: Yes.

DIANE: Small world, huh?

KATHERINE: Oh my God! That's so weird! How did you know her?

JOHN: Well it's sort of a, sort of a, long story.

EDMUND: They used to live together.

KATHERINE: What do you mean?

JOHN: We lived together.

KATHERINE: What? Really? Dad, how did you… Edmund…you didn't know about this, did you?

JOHN: Apparently he did.

KATHERINE: What? You knew?

DIANE: Kath, honey—

KATHERINE: What's going on here? I mean, what the— you knew about this Edmund and never—

JOHN: He never told you because it was to his advantage not to. Edmund is…well, like I said earlier, Edmund is a measurer. He measures out precisely—and I admit I'm guessing, I've only just met him—but he measures out pretty much everything he does. Everything he says and to whom he says it. Including—especially you.

EDMUND: No different than you, John, I'm sure.

JOHN: You're sure of this, are you Edmund? That's a word I'd be very careful with if I were you. I'd be very careful about all your words these next few minutes. One poet to another.

DIANE: Edmund, please, not like this. This isn't fair to her.

KATHERINE: I don't understand. Any of this. Edmund, what's going on?

EDMUND: We've been talking about my mother.

KATHERINE: Your mother?

EDMUND: I've told you about her, about—all the stuff she put me through, put herself through. But I never told you about her notebooks.

KATHERINE: What notebooks?

EDMUND: My mother kept a safety deposit box and on my 21st birthday I was given the key.

JOHN: The point?

KATHERINE: Dad, please. What, Edmund?

EDMUND: I put the key in a drawer and pretended to ignore it. Three years it sits there because the nicest tribute I could pay my mother was to try to forget she ever existed. But the harder I tried, the larger it loomed; she loomed. So I say to myself—fuck it, get it overwith. And it's notebooks. In her handwriting. And what she wrote…for the first time in my experience with her—coherent. In fact, beautiful. And filled with your father's poetry.

KATHERINE: My father's?

JOHN: Is that what you're basing it on? Notebooks?

EDMUND: These notebooks were deposited, I later found out, the week your father's second book came out. A year before the third. And nearly ten before the fourth.

JOHN: Diane.

EDMUND: They had poems from all four of your father's books. My mother's poetry in his books.

KATHERINE: Edmund, what are you, you implying?

JOHN: He's not implying. He's staking his claim. Edmund thinks I stole all of my poems from his mother.

KATHERINE: Edmund is that, is that true? *(Silence)* What's happening here?

JOHN: What's happening is he's used you, sweetheart. To get to me. He's lied to and used you in a way that is simply breathtaking. I'm sorry.

KATHERINE: Jesus, Edmund...oh my God, did you— you planned this? You planned this? Say something. Say something. Oh my God.

DIANE: Sweetheart.

KATHERINE: No, Mom, —Jesus, you planned this. I'm such an idiot.

JOHN:	DIANE:
No sweetheart.	Of course not.

KATHERINE: You used me.

DIANE: Katherine.

KATHERINE: What were you thinking? When we met? When you, you touched me?

EDMUND: Your father.

KATHERINE: Jesus.

EDMUND: When I read those notebooks, I, I right away recognize a couple of the poems. They're different enough not to have been copied by rote, but they're there, the same...spine, same heartbeat. So I go to the bookstore, find your father's books and sit on the floor: I sit there for two hours. By the time the manager tells me I have to leave, I know the whole story.

JOHN: That's the root of this? Jesus, Edmund.

EDMUND: And when we met, and I heard you talk about him, saw your face, your face *glow* whenever you mentioned him…I knew: you were going to be the way. That's what I was thinking that first night.

JOHN: Jesus, Edmund, is this is the opera you've orchestrated in your mind—the cruelty to my daughter? Of *course* she had copies of my poems. Of course she did. Of course she had them before they were published. All my books had at least a few poems from that time and I always gave your mother copies of my poems. *Always* We *lived* together, remember? My God, I certainly hope if you're so hellbent on burning my family, you've brought better kindling than notebooks.

EDMUND: Not *copies*—drafts, revisions—

JOHN: Scribbling. Fragments—she was losing her mind. Bet you there's scraps of Walt Whitman in there, too --- she loved him. Think she gave him *Leaves of Grass?*

EDMUND: Katherine, I don't expect you to forgive me. But look at the facts.

DIANE: We are, Edmund. Turns out they're not the allies you thought they were.

EDMUND: God, Katherine: They lied to you about the circumstances of coming home for your father's *birth*day, Katherine, right?

KATHERINE: *(She goes to* JOHN. DIANE *goes to the two of them.* EDMUND *sees them as a unit.)* Stay the fuck away from my family. I hope you end up just like her. I want him to know he's wrong, that he's been…been wrong, Dad. Deluded his, his whole life, like his *fucking mother!*

JOHN: O K. Let's calm down.

KATHERINE: I am calm. I'm a fucking *buddha.*

JOHN: Did she ever call me a thief?

EDMUND: What?

JOHN: In the notebooks. Did she accuse me of stealing poetry?

EDMUND: Not directly.

JOHN: Not directly? She imply I stole them?

EDMUND: She…she showed me what she gave you.

JOHN: No mention of theft. Then why are you here? Why did we ever have to endure the trauma of knowing you? Whatever words or phrases she gave me, I wrote the poetry. And your mother never disputes that. Are we done?

KATHERINE: Dad?

JOHN: What, sweetheart?

KATHERINE: What does that mean? "Gave." *(Pause)* What are you saying? That she—

JOHN: *(Over "That she—")* Just that.

KATHERINE: She gave you words?

EDMUND: Many.

KATHERINE: *(To* EDMUND*)* Shut up. I am talking to my father. She *gave* you words?

JOHN: Sweetheart, you're not seriously—you can't expect me to go back over each poem forensically. We were two young poets living together. You can't expect artists, artists who are intimate at all with each other, not to share. You're a poet, Katherine, you understand.

KATHERINE: We share. You've never given me words.

JOHN: Katherine, I know he's put you through—

KATHERINE: It's not about him or what he said. I mean you and I talked all my *life* about—we've gone through every poem. But you never mentioned her. So talk to me now. Please.

EDMUND: You ever talk about "The River Cluster"?

JOHN: What?

EDMUND: Don't be so humble: "The River Cluster", the famous one from your second book. The one all the high school textbooks have.

KATHERINE: Just—Jesus, go away, what *about* it?

JOHN: Kath—

EDMUND: Named after the group of dorms you lived in, right, John? That Kath lived in—til recently, anyway, because of that need you instilled in her to follow in your footsteps step by pathologically needy step. Anyway, "The River Cluster": Famously sad and sweet memories of your college days, eh? Tell me— either of you—in your conversations about it, did you guys ever talk about why it seems to be written from the perspective of an outsider? A townie, almost?

JOHN: You're in even worse shape than I thought if you think I'm going to discuss—

EDMUND: Why do the students seem older and more knowing than the speaker, one has to wonder? I'm sure, John, that you bullshitted something clever about alienation and irony, about speaker versus writer, but doesn't it feel like the speaker *grew up* watching these people? I mean, that's the beauty of the poem really, its central throbbing ache—watching them from a distance rather than, you know, *being* one of them? The voice of the townie, the outsider—that's the one that you get so right, the one the critics swoon over, the voice that haunts and gets quoted in yearbooks. And of course, that was *Zora*. Her life, her *voice*, wasn't it? It was your college, John, but Zora's hometown, wasn't it?

JOHN: Arthur Miller didn't kill himself after getting fired from his sales job, either, and yet so many of us still naively cling to the belief that he wrote *Death of a Salesman*. This is idictic. *(To* KATHERINE *now)* Sweetheart.

KATHERINE: Dad, just tell me about her, tell me — please just explain to me—

JOHN: *(Over her "please")* My God, Katherine. Has he somehow got me defending myself to *you*— He's *admitted* he's lied to you—Katherine!

KATHERINE: It's not about him—he's doesn't—

JOHN: *(Over "about him")* And he's been lying to you all along, trying to sand the edges off of his ruthlessness, but everything you thought you had with him's a lie. Deny it, Edmund, let's see how good you really are— look her in the eyes again and deny it.

EDMUND: This is a misdirection, not surprising, given his whole life's a conjuring act. You look your daughter in the eye and deny that.

JOHN: I can refute your assertions and it won't make a difference to you, will it? The irony is your mother was the same way. Couldn't talk her out of anything once she made her mind up. But you've known for a while you and your mother are alike. You see it, right? More vitally, you feel it, don't you?

EDMUND: You're not going to distract us.

JOHN: From what? Your *argument?* This is the *point*: your *thought process. (Beat)* You claim to want to bring out the truth. Well here it comes. Your mother wasn't in control of herself.

EDMUND: You think you're going to educate me on my mother's—

JOHN: She wasn't in control of herself, she slept with anyone who'd smile at her, anyone who gave her correct change, but not to hurt me or…it was a symptom, her behavior. Just like tonight is for you, of course. It was after we'd started to share a life, after the humiliations of her promiscuity and her rages and paranoia and the, the intense gravity of her despair. That we realized she was sick. And she wasn't going to get better. Was going to, in fact, get a lot worse. She never wanted to have children, of course; she didn't want to run the risk of passing it on. But of course she wasn't much in control of herself by the time I had to leave her. And you're proof of that continued descent, aren't you? In her right mind, she never would've allowed herself to give birth to you; can you understand that? Your existence is a monument to her disease. But here you are, just as angry and sad and just as, you must realize by now, lost.

DIANE: John.

JOHN: You figure: now or never. Make a missile out of your life and aim it at my family. *(Pause)* Again, no denial.

KATHERINE: *(Uneasy with* JOHN's *hardness)* Dad.

JOHN: Katherine, this is what he is; it's all he is. It's important to name it and know it.

EDMUND: *(Struggling not to seem shaken)* That doesn't change what you've done.

JOHN: What you think I've done. What you think you've proven, it's nonsense. Provable by the fact that your mind, that sad little mechanism stripping its gears in front of our eyes, believes it so totally.

DIANE: John. Katherine.

KATHERINE: Dad. Please.

JOHN: What? I'm supposed to feign contrition or some sort of, of vague theoretical culpability because this sick boy's got a notion? Let him try to destroy my career and reputation? Humiliate you? That you could be fooled by that?

KATHERINE: Dad, please just —

JOHN: This is ridiculous, Katherine. I deserve your mistrust? —tonight of all nights? Made poet laureate and ambushed in my home—how do I deserve that in your mind?

KATHERINE: No—no—I just think—

JOHN: I'm your father— I've earned your trust.

KATHERINE: I do trust you; I want to.

JOHN: You want to?

DIANE: Katherine, let's talk about this later—

KATHERINE: But you said they're her words.

JOHN: They're everyone's words! Zora's. Yours. Your mother's, Shakespeare's, John Lennon's, David Letterman's for God's sake.

KATHERINE: But I've heard you mention them. Never her.

JOHN: *(Over "her")* They're everyone's words for the taking, and yes, I take them—without apology—and shape them into poems—

KATHERINE: Poems that I have worshipped.

DIANE: Katherine, you can't expect your father—

KATHERINE: You watched me bang my head against the wall of those poems all my life.

JOHN: Sweetheart.

KATHERINE: *(Over her mother's words)* I hounded you for any scrap of inspiration—and all you'd say is "wouldn't it be nice if that could be taught."

JOHN: Is it because I can do it and you can't? Is that what this is, finally, Katherine? If you believe anything this diseased boy you let into your bed and my home is spewing, it's because there's part of you that wants to. Don't, sweetheart. And if a few words extracted from the rubble of that sick woman's mind —

KATHERINE: Dad.

JOHN: Jesus Christ, Katherine, enough. You somehow think I deserve to stand here and have my life, and my work, my work, audited? By him or you or anyone? I was the one who made them into poems. Even if some, some of the word or phrases—some—are hers, the poems are mine.

(JOHN *sees* KATHERINE *looking at him. Off of her look:*)

JOHN: They are, Katherine, they—saying those poems are hers is like saying the workman who hauled the block of stone Michelangelo used was really the one who made the statue of David.

KATHERINE: Dad, that's...that's...

JOHN: *(A flash of searing, explosive anger overtakes him)* The poems ARE MINE, GODDAMMIT!

(Silence. Stillness. The doorbell rings. Pause. Doorbell rings again.)

DIANE: John. You have to get the door now.

(Doorbell rings again.)

JOHN: Yes.

DIANE: Tell them we'll be out in a minute.

(JOHN, in a daze at was has just happened, walk towards the exit. Stops: to DIANE, gesturing towards EDMUND)

JOHN: Fine. I will. I want him out of the house now. Clear? Now. I don't care how or—get him out. Do you understand?

(The doorbell rings. Pause)

DIANE: Go on. We'll be out in a—go on.

(DIANE *and* JOHN *look at each other*)

DIANE: Go.

(JOHN *exits. Silence*)

EDMUND: Kath—

KATHERINE: No. No fucking speech. You should've just told me.

EDMUND: You would never have believed me.

KATHERINE: How can I believe you now?

(*Pause.* EDMUND *goes upstage, gets his jacket and knapsack.*)

EDMUND: I'm gonna be pushed to the side pretty quickly, I imagine. By you and John. By everyone, maybe. (*He puts the knapsack on the coffee table. Beat: this is important: to* KATHERINE) But you wouldn't be; you can't be. Look at it yourself.

KATHERINE: Fuck you.

EDMUND: If your father's right, you've nothing to lose. Look at it yourself.

(EDMUND *tries to give* KATHERINE *the knapsack. She refuses. He puts the knapsack down near her.*)

EDMUND: These are yours. Now.

(*Pause.* EDMUND *and* KATHERINE *look at each other. He turns from her, starts to exit.*)

EDMUND: These weren't things he overheard in a café that stuck with him. (*He gently picks up the knapsack and places it back on the coffee table.*) These were expressions of—expressions of great intimacy she *gave* to him. As gifts. You have your parents and your, your obligations. And I have mine. So.

(EDMUND *picks up the bag, places it gently on the floor, not too near her, but visible. He exits.* KATHERINE'S *reserves of composure desert her, and she moves to the center stage couch, deeply shaken.* DIANE *moves to her, wanting to comfort but unsure of how.)*

DIANE: I'm… Katherine. Katherine I'm so…sorry.

KATHERINE: What are we…what's going to happen?

DIANE: I haven't a clue, my baby. Not a clue.

KATHERINE: I can't believe he…

DIANE: I know; he's gone now.

KATHERINE: No. Both of them.

DIANE: Sweetheart…your father loves you very much. I love you very much.

(KATHERINE *nods.)*

DIANE: But you've always held him up to be so… It doesn't help anyone, to hang onto that, you see? But past a certain point… You're such a smart young thing, I'd always assumed you'd get that on your own. But you've always been so…devout. Your father loves you. That's the most important thing, right? That's enough. It's all you can know for certain…it has to be enough.

(Pause)

(DIANE *and* KATHERINE *look at each other. Pause.* KATHERINE *reaches a decision. She then stands and retrieves the knapsack.)*

DIANE: Katherine, please—not tonight, sweetheart. Not—

KATHERINE: It's O K.

(JOHN *enters.* KATHERINE *looks at* JOHN *but does not stop; she takes the knapsack and passes them both on the way back to her room.)*

JOHN: Katherine. Sweetheart.

(DIANE *and* KATHERINE *look at each other once more.* DIANE *and* JOHN *lock eyes.* KATHERINE *looks at* JOHN,

then to DIANE. *They look at one another,* JOHN *and* DIANE
downstage and flanking KATHERINE, *who is upstage and*
holds the knapsack, ready to go to her room.)

END OF PLAY

www.ingramcontent.com/pod-product-compliance
Lightning Source LLC
Chambersburg PA
CBHW052217090426
42741CB00010B/2577